DIVINE PATTERNS OF SACRED GEOMETRY

Kanakolu Press
Carlsbad, California

Copyright © Deborah DeLisi
www.DeLisiArt.com
USA

ISBN-13: 978-0692659700
ISBN-10: 0692659706

CURATED COLORING BOOKS™ : VOLUME 1

DIVINE PATTERNS OF SACRED GEOMETRY

For Intuitive Connection & Mindful Relaxation

Deborah DeLisi

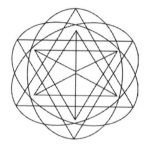

Sacred Geometry is an ancient tool for discovering the creation and order of all things, through which our ancestors pondered the arrangement of our world and universe. By combining mathematics, science and intuitive awareness, they formed beliefs about the world around them. The language of mathematics, then and now, has a quality that expresses relationships in order to reveal the structure and orderly principles of the world around us. These relationships often manifest as patterns that allow us to discover the nature and power of the force that makes all things. Allow these 33 divine patterns to speak to your "inner realm," the sacred place within. Let the ancient forms guide your meditation and awareness. Relax and enjoy coloring each page as you unlock the ancient wisdom of Sacred Geometry.

Kanakolu Press

Fractals

A fractal is a self-similar mathematical pattern that can repeat infinitely. The word *fractal* was coined by mathematician Benoit Mandelbrot (1924-2010), who introduced the idea as a way to use math to measure irregular land contours like a shoreline or geometric figure. He put forth the idea that seemingly chaotic things actually contain a mathematical order. In the **Mandelbrot Set** shown at right, each part has the same statistical character as the whole.

It is interesting to ponder that humans may be a type of fractal. We are reproduced from human parents, and in turn, give birth to human forms (children) capable of repeating this fractal infinitely.

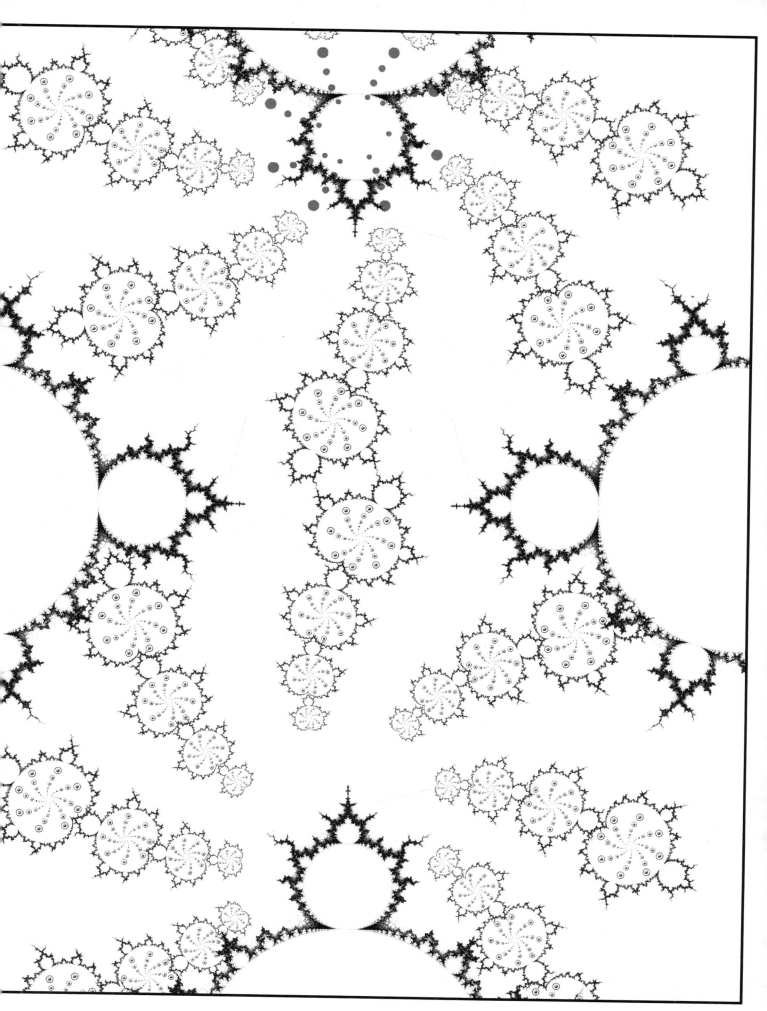

Sun & Moon Mandala

▶

A mandala is a spiritual vehicle that arose thousands of years ago to teach sacred texts and pass on knowledge about the order of our world. As symbols, they embody the interrelationships and common source between all things in the universe, representing oneness.

The **Sun & Moon Mandala** depicts the dance of push and pull between the sun, moon and earth, which causes the rise and fall of the tides and cycles of day and night. Such cycles have existed since long before our distant ancestors walked the earth. The symbol in the center conveys an ancient connection to the Pleaides *Seven Sisters* constellation and an esoteric belief that ancient humans were seeded by them.

Sierpinski Triangle

▶

This type of triangular fractal was described by mathematician Waclaw Sierpinski in 1915. It can elegantly replicate itself, expanding inward and outward infinitely. To create this pattern, reduce width and height by half, then triplicate the shape and place it so that each corner touches the other 2 triangles. This depiction of the **Sierpinski Triangle** is in the shape of a 3D Star Tetrahedron. Is it math, engineering, art or sacred geometry? Like our world, it is all of the above. Humans have long been fascinated by this motif, and it can be found as far back as the 13th century in Italian church mosaics.

Sri Yantra

The **Sri Yantra** is Buddhist in origin, reaching back over 10,000 years, and is said to have to have a powerful effect on the subtle energy body. It is known as the geometry of self-realization and is to be viewed as having depth and dimension rather than a flat plane. The four upward triangles represent the MALE god Shiva, and five downward triangles represent the FEMALE goddess Shakti. It is the dance of creation, the union and balance of male and female, with the central point being the source from where the universe sprang. Although the geometries may look askew, each triangle is constructed from very exacting measurements.

The Seed of Life

There is much to ponder in the symbolism of the seven interlocking circles that form a flower. The circle is considered the perfect geometry: whole, containing everything and without beginning or end. The center of **The Seed of Life** flower creates a point from which all else grows. The Pythagoreans felt that everything starts with a point, and when it is infused with love, it expands into the sphere. From there, everything procreates, like the fertilized egg. **The Seed of Life** can also be viewed as symbolic of the creation story of a God who made our world in six days, and on the seventh day, being pleased with his/her creation, rested.

THE FLOWER OF LIFE

As The Seed of Life (previous page) grows in progression, it forms the symbol known as **The Flower of Life**. This ancient geometry has been found in the 6000-year-old Temple of Osiris in Abydos, Egypt, as well as in archaeological sites in China, Israel, Japan, India, Turkey, Italy and Spain. Even Leonardo da Vinci sketched and pondered this shape in his famous Codex Atlanticus drawings. It is an intriguing form that makes one aware of the interconnectedness of all things in the microcosm and macrocosm, the oneness in the many and the order of harmony and balance.

Metatron's Cube

Metatron is an angel of Rabbinic traditions and is said to be God's scribe, or "The One Who Sits Next to the One on the Throne." The geometric shape named after Metatron is made of 13 circles from the Flower of Life (previous page). These 13 circles are also called The Fruit of Life: the blueprint of the universe. In **Metatron's Cube** each circle is connected to all other circles at the center point. Through this geometry of interconnectedness, numerous incredible shapes appear. All five of the Platonic Solids (at the bottom of the drawing) can be found nested within Metatron's Cube.

The 5 Platonic Solids

Don't be fooled by their name, the **Platonic Solids** were known long before Plato. The Pythagoreans knew these geometric forms as the Mathematical Solids, and each must meet specific criteria: 1) they are regular polyhedrons (a geometric solids in three dimensions with flat faces and straight edges); 2) they are identical on each side, and; 3) they have the same number of faces meeting at each vertex. Only five shapes meet this criteria— (*clockwise*) the tetrahedron, octahedron, icosahedron, dodecahedron and hexahedron (or cube).

The 5 Platonic Solids

Set against the backdrop of Mt. Shasta, California, **The 5 Platonic Solids** seem to float through space and time. Each Platonic Solid is associated with an element. The tetrahedron points upward like a flame and is **FIRE**. An octahedron balances on a point and seems to float, like **AIR**. The icosahedron rolls off a hand like **WATER**. The square hexahedron indicates movement of the four directions we navigate by: left, right, forward or backward, and symbolizes **EARTH**. And lastly, the dodecahedron is associated with **ETHER** which Pythagoras said was the element the heavens are made of.

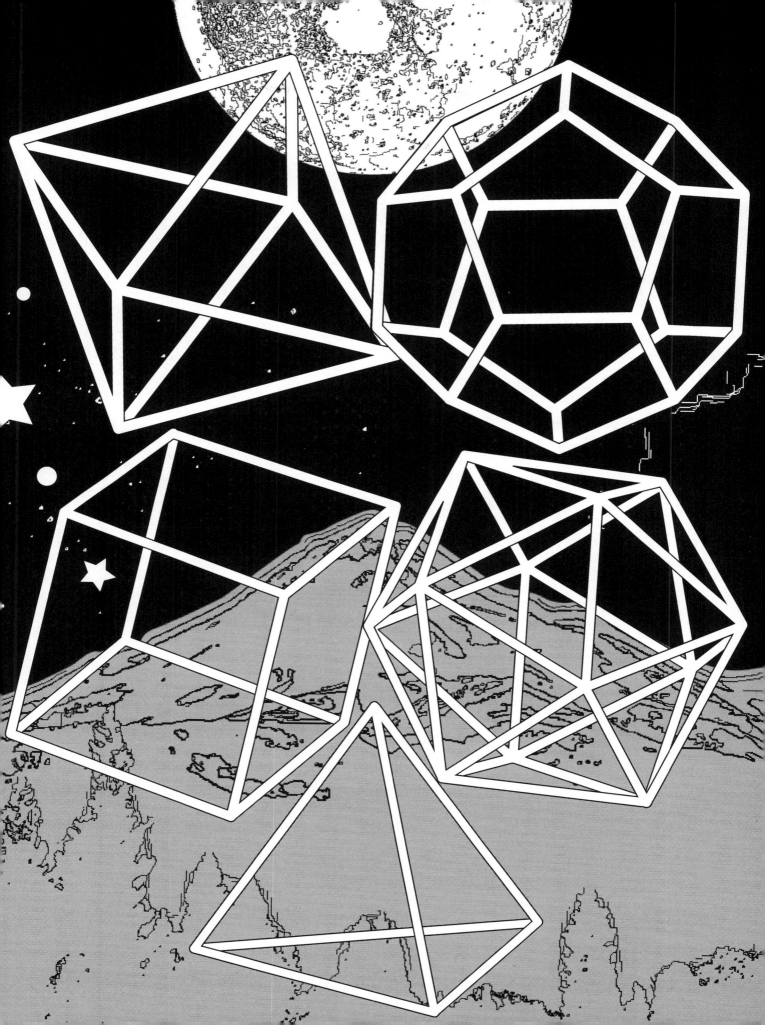

The Pythagorean Tetractys

Pythagoras had a school 500 years before Christ and spent nearly three decades studying in Egypt before starting his "Brotherhood" in southern Italy. Inclusive of both men and women, their main discipline was mathematics, although each day began and ended with song and music. Their revered **Tetractys** was an expression of a mathematical idea as well as a holy symbol for the Pythagoreans. They saw the tetrad as containing the order of nature with its four stacked rows of triangles, symbolizing 1+2+3+4=10, the decad, after which all number repeats.

Each row was associated with a dimension: 1st= an "unbegotten number," still part of wholeness; (the zero dimension of a point); 2nd= the one-dimension (a line of two points) and the separation from unity; 3rd= 3=synthesis, creation and the 2nd dimension of a plane (triangle). The 4th row = order, structure, perfection and the 3rd dimension of a tetrahedron (defined by 4 points).

Pythagorean Tree

The **Pythagorean Tree** is a modern mathematical construct that is a plane fractal constructed from squares. Invented by the Dutch mathematics teacher, Albert E. Bosman in 1942, it's named after Pythagoras because each triple of the squares produces a Pythagorean triangle. This is a beautiful artistic expression of pure math, repeating itself into form, and speaks to our inner understanding of how life can be built from order. Is it a tree, a brain and spinal cord, or something else? You decide! Ponder it as you use color to bring it to life.

Metta Mandala

In the scriptural Pali language of India, "Metta" means loving kindness. It expresses the love of one who deeply cares for another and takes action to bring that
kindness outward. Buddha said, "A beautiful word or thought which is not accompanied by corresponding acts is like a bright flower which bears no fruit. It would
not produce any effect."

My **Metta Mandala** design was created to express a radiating love that one can
take action on, permeating kindness for self, for another and for the world.

CROP CIRCLE MANDALA ▶

Whether they're made by people or extraterrestrial visitors, the intricate patterns of crop circles are dazzling geometric creations. Each design can be contemplated for meaning, its messages conveyed in the symbolic language of mathematical precision. This **Crop Circle Mandala** was inspired by one that appeared near Windmill Hill, Wiltshire in the United Kingdom. This design is pentagonal geometry instead of the original hexagonal crop circle layout. Enjoy exploring personal meaning while coloring this mandala.

Triskelion Crop Circle ▶

Wiltshire, England boasts many crop circles spanning several decades. One of the most famous was the design on the right which appeared in 2001. The geometry is a variation of a Celtic symbol called a triskelion, which looks like three running legs or spirals radiating from a center. This double **Triskelion Crop Circle** was enormous—over 780 feet (238 meters)—and had over 400 circles. My interpretation of this crop circle has over 600 circles in the main design, and even more floating around it. Enjoy the relaxation of coloring this and making it come to life on the page!

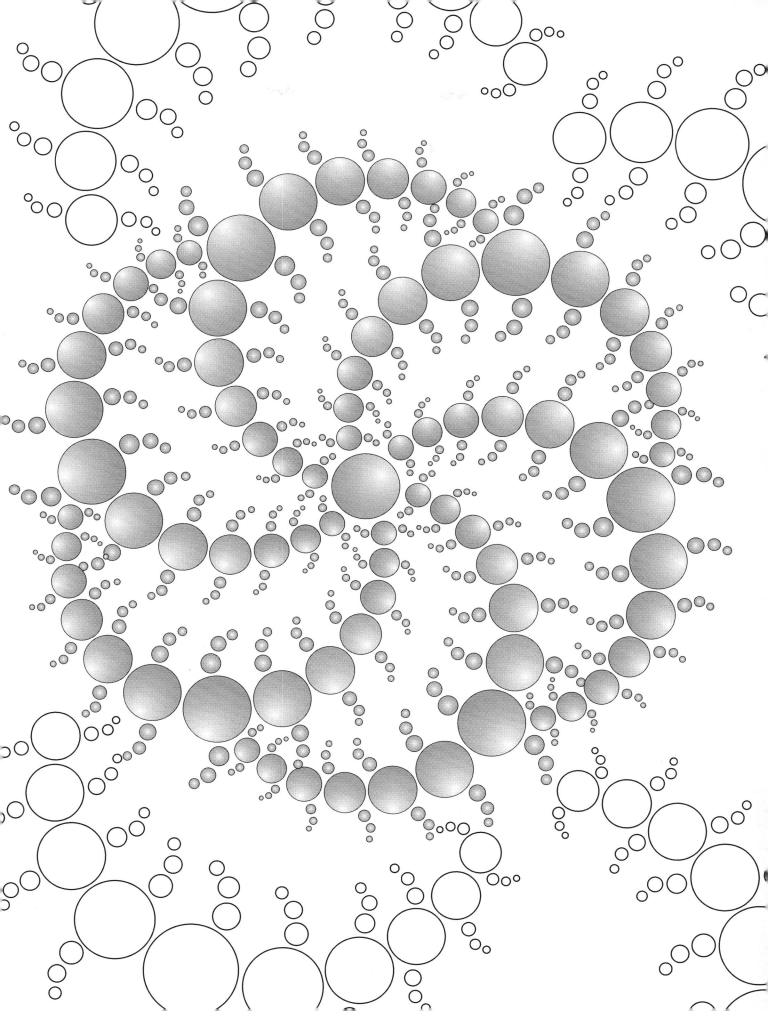

Crown Chakra: Violet
The highest level of consciousness and enlightenment, the connective center to spirit.

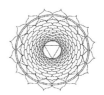

Third Eye Chakra: Indigo
The place of intuition, visionary seeing and spiritual awakening.

Throat Chakra: Light Blue
The center for self-expression, speaking our truth.

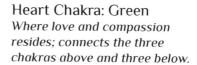

Heart Chakra: Green
Where love and compassion resides; connects the three chakras above and three below.

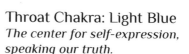

Solar Plexus Chakra: Yellow
The center for personal power, located above the navel.

Sacral Chakra: Orange
The center of creativity and sexuality, just below the navel.

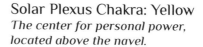

Root Chakra: Red
At the base of the spine, and related to survival, stability & grounding.

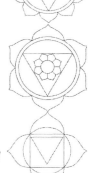

The Chakras

▶

Approximately 1,000 years ago in India, Vedic texts and oral traditions described energy centers in the body, known as the **Chakras,** or wheels that were made of the life force. There are seven main centers in the body, aligned from the top of the head to the base of the spine. Each is associated with a physical purpose and a color. The symbols shown come from Sanskrit traditions, with each corresponding color and basic meaning shown above.

Durga Yantra

A yantra is a Hindu mandala that is a visual prayer to god or goddess. Durga is a Hindu deity and fierce warrior goddess whose role was to fight the buffalo-demon Mahishasura, a monster too powerful for man and god. The **Durga Yantra** is said to offer protection from one's enemies and assist in achieving victory, embodying courage and expressing the strength of mother-goddess energy.

Although not part of the traditional Durga Yantra, the flower symbols placed in each corner contain meaning. Each contains six perfect circles, a number associated with creation, love, harmony and balance. Even numbers are considered to be feminine, and six holds that energy.

Ganesha Yantra

Ganesha is a popular Buddhist deity who was assimilated into Hinduism too. He has the head of an elephant, a human body and is usually depicted dancing, sitting or reclining. Although there are many variants of the meaning of Ganesha, his powers are very helpful in removing obstacles, aiding in successful business ventures and new beginnings. This **Ganesha Yantra** of geometric symbolism has been around many centuries and is a visual tool for contemplating and focusing on this elephant deity so that benevolent blessings may grace you.

The Third Eye of Intuitive Connection ▶

Located between the eyebrows and slightly above, the **Third Eye Chakra** is long thought to be a source of inner insights and visions and a portal to the invisible realms. It takes one beyond the limits of what the eyes can see and into the land of mystical wisdom. Accessing the Third Eye requires meditation and practice, just as connecting to intuition does. As you color this ancient being in a meditative state, use your third eye to bring awareness to information that may come through.

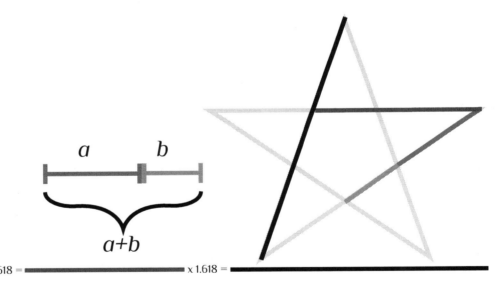

a b

$a+b$

⬛⬛⬛ x 1.618 = ⬛⬛⬛⬛ x 1.618 = ⬛⬛⬛⬛⬛⬛ x 1.618 = ⬛⬛⬛⬛⬛⬛⬛⬛⬛

The Golden Ratio Spiral ▶

More than any other number, the **Golden Ratio** has inspired mathematicians, biologists, artists, musicians, architects and mystics. The formula is: *a+b is to a as a is to b*. There you have a golden ratio, of 1:1.618. On the far right, each square multiplies by 1.618 and "grows". The arched line from corner to corner creates the expanding pattern known as the golden spiral. It is similar to cell division or fractals, where dividing the "parent" and reproducing a "child" identical to the parent could go on infinitely.

Level One: The Seed of Creation

In 2005 I started creating art that was seen in my third eye when certain "pineal tones" were sung by a friend and collaborator. **Level One** is the first in that series (The Art of the Pineal Tones) and represents "a spark igniting the seed of creation." Water and light stimulate the seed of creative consciousness to expand awareness of a divine source. The geometries represent the seeding of codes that are building blocks and the geometric underpinnings of the universe. You may meditate on this while coloring: "I am now a channel of light and I radiate the expression of my creator. I remember my divine eternal perfection."

Fractal Star of Abundance ▶

I intuitively saw this star symbol along with the word "abundance" and this meaning: "When you hear the word **ABUNDANCE** it can conjure up thoughts of *lots of money*. True, but it can mean so much more than that. Don't limit abundance! It can also mean an abundance of HEALTH for you, an abundance of LOVING RELATIONSHIPS IN YOUR LIFE, an abundance of PEACE IN YOUR WORLD, an abundance of FREEDOM, an abundance of OPPORTUNITIES THAT ARE PRESENTED TO YOU, an abundance of TIME TO CREATE WHAT YOU DESIRE and an abundance of SUPPORT for what you're going through." The word Abundance is truly dimensional and has many aspects to it. Allow the geometries of abundance to support you in the way you choose.

The Merkabah

▶

The symbol of an upward triangle imposed over a downward facing triangle has many meanings. As the Star of David it's the symbol for the Jewish faith and served as a protective device, worn on the ring of King Solomon and imbued with special powers. This symbol is also **The Merkabah**, meaning "to ride" as in a chariot in Hebrew. Mer-Ka-Bah = Light-spirit-soul. It's thought to transport us— or our light body vehicle— from one dimension to another. The Merkabah also represents a state of balance between man/god, male/female and is the Hindu symbol for the heart chakra.

Octahedron Mandala

The beauty of the **Octahedron** and the numerology of the eight sides is the inspiration for this mandala. An octahedron is one of the Platonic Solids and is made by doubling the rhombic pyramid, which has four sides. As a geometric shape, it is beautifully balanced, and perhaps that is why the Pythagoreans called eight the *number of justice*. Pythagoras said that in the symbol of an eight we find an expression of the eternal spiral motion of cycles, the regular in-breathing and out-breathing of the Great Breath. It is a place where struggle is absent. In numerology, eight is associated with good fortune, prosperity, abundance and wealth.

The Sacred Egyptian Scarab

▶

The winged scarab is symbolic of the dung beetle which lays its eggs in dung balls fashioned through rolling. This beetle was associated with the divine manifestation of the early morning sun and a hieroglyphic symbol for Khepri, the creator god responsible for the movement of the sun. Like the symbolic beetle who disappeared into the earth only to re-emerge, Khepri was believed to roll the morning sun over the horizon at daybreak. The winged scarab was worn as a protective amulet on mummies. It was believed to make the heart of the deceased lighter when weighed against Ma'at's "feather of truth," assuring that Osiris would grant them passage into the afterworld.

The Tree of Life ▶

The **Tree of Life** symbol appears in many forms, cultures and religions. The one shown here is the Kabbalistic symbol and a geometry for mystic thought and insights into life and the balance of creation. The left side represents the female aspect of: judgment, understanding, severity and glory. On the right is the male aspect: wisdom, love, mercy and victory. The middle is the balance between male and female and symbolizes the harmony of the source, beauty, union and kingdom. These three forces—female, male and harmony—represent opposites, with balance or neutrality in the middle. As these forces co-mingle, creation manifests.

Sunflower Mandala

▶

Like the expanding center spiral of a sunflower, this mandala moves one outward while also focusing inward and back to the point in the center. There is much to ponder while coloring this design, and please allow the colors to be spontaneous as the joy of this sunflower unfolds in a way uniquely yours.

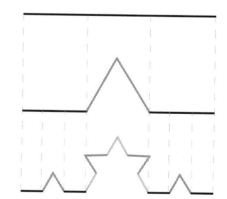

The "Koch Snowflake" Fractal

In 1906, Swedish math professor Niels Fabian Helge von Koch published a paper describing what is known as the Koch curve. It is constructed by dividing a line into three equal parts, then replacing the middle segment by the other two sides of an equilateral triangle constructed on the middle segment. This fractal pattern can repeat indefinitely. When you start with an equilateral triangle instead of a line, the fractal shape that forms is known as a **Koch Snowflake** or star.

The Toroid

A **Toroid** is a word to describe a donut-shaped figure. In certain areas of physics, the toroid is considered to be the perfect shape, due to its efficient configuration for generation of power and storage. Some theories claim the universe is a toroid, the perfect shape for balance energy flow. The top image is toroid and below is an aerial view of the same form. The small shape is made of two triple-toroids, called a torus knot, that are stacked and rotated at 60°.

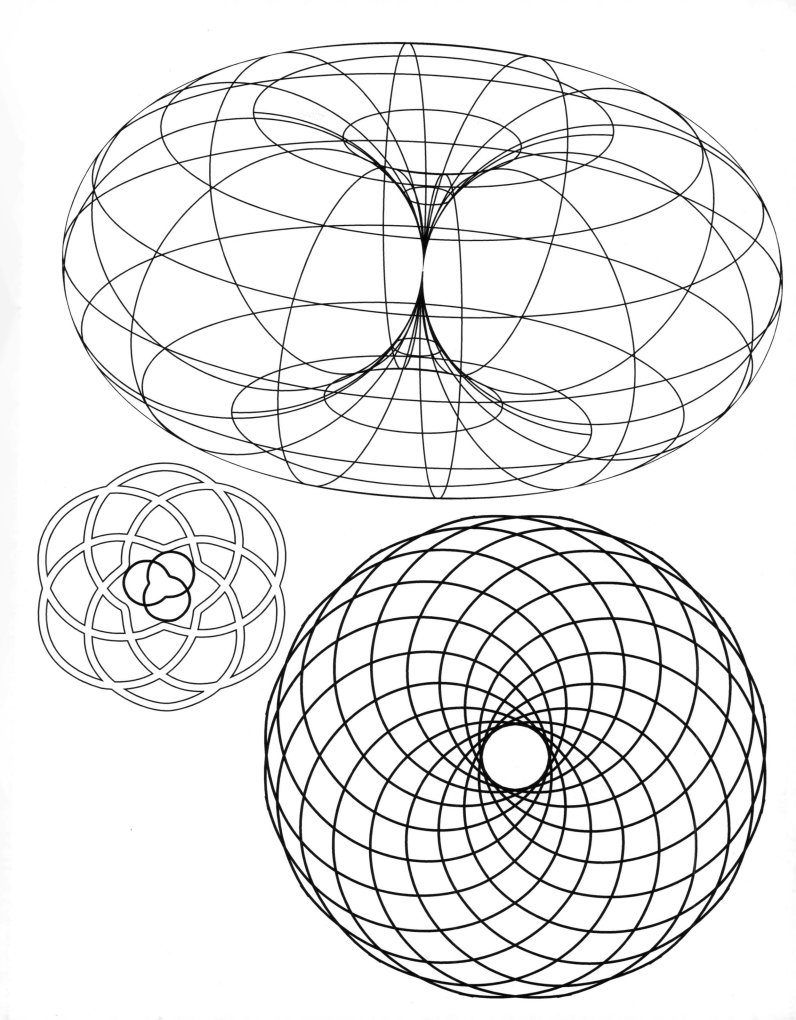

Light Language

Light Language is spoken and/or written by intuitive channelers around the world. It's neither new nor old and isn't documented as being part of a specific culture, region or time period. The language has a timeless appeal and is expressed uniquely by each channeler, using many sounds and symbols, sometimes accompanied by hand movements that bring in energy. Each transmission of this energetic language carries encodements and frequencies that activate soul memories and one's DNA. The languages are thought to come from various sources: angels, intergalactic beings, earth elementals and other dimensional beings.

The Toroid Knot

This illustration expresses the helical movement of the **Toroid Knot** and the Moebius energy that moves evenly both inward and outward. It's easy to see how this shape may be related to the way our energy field moves within and without our bodies, as well as how our heart beats and our universe pulses.

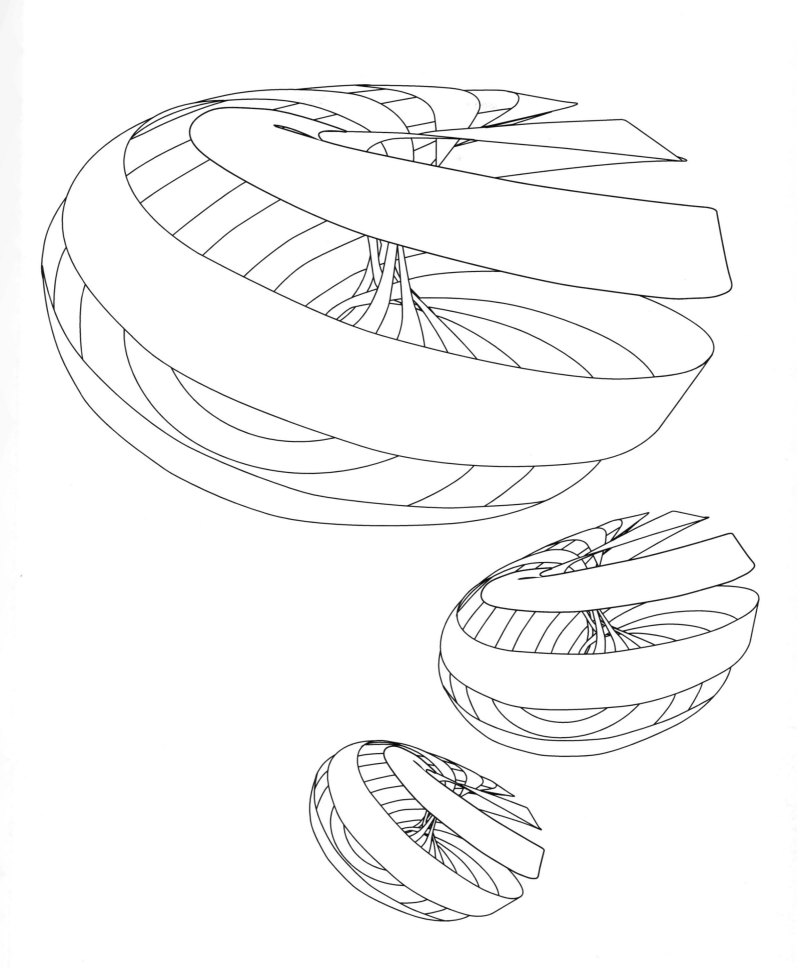

Our DNA

Deoxyribonucleic Acid (**DNA**) is the biological structural code that makes you who you are. DNA forms a helix pattern. The two strands form a "twisted ladder" of information that is unique to every living being. The helix is an efficient shape for stacking base pairs that can replicate themselves ensuring the survival of the species. The twist in it solves the problem of having parts of it "bump" into each other.

DNA Mandala

▶

It is theorized that less than 10% of our **DNA** seems to be doing something functional, as related to our biology and physiology. So what does the other 90% do? There is esoteric thinking that postulates our DNA has quantum or interdimensional functions not understood in 3D. If the majority of DNA has no purpose, how did it survive the evolutionary process that benefits us? Some say that our DNA holds quantum information that remembers the lifetimes of our soul and also connects each individual to the larger universe. It's an interesting theory that may prove to have merit. This mandala expresses DNA as 12 strands, forming a geometry of communication. Enjoy pondering the possibilities within you as you color!

The Fibonacci Sequence ▶

Italian mathematician from Pisa, Leonardo Bonaccio (c. 1175-1245), is known as "Fibonacci," short for *filius* (son of) Bonaccio. Because his father was a trading agent in North Africa, he was educated under the Moors influence. Later, he became a pioneer in introducing the Hindu-Arabic system (1, 2, 3, 4, 5, 6, 7, 8, 9, 0) of writing numbers to Europe, replacing Roman numerals. In his book he posed and solved a mathematical problem of the growth of rabbit populations with his **Fibonacci Sequence**: *a series of numbers in which each number is the sum of the two numbers before it.* 1,1,2,3,5,8,13,21,34,55,89...and so on. Much later, this mathematical pattern was found in nature. If you look at the crisscross spiral in the center of a sunflower, the number of spirals in each direction are usually two consecutive Fibonacci numbers. This pattern is also found in pine cones, shell spirals and the way plants put out new shoots, to name a few.

Made in the USA
San Bernardino, CA
09 March 2017